Finding God's Goodness in Unexpected Places challenged me personally to keep looking for God, noticing His presence in the ups and downs of life. Angela shares her story openly and with great vulnerability. She challenges me to press in and not to let difficulties defeat me. Through the questions at the end of the chapter, she helped me look at my own life and be intentional in seeing God's presence and work in me. This is a wonderful book that helps us to keep on looking for God Himself.

Monika Nadig, University of the
Nations – Cambodia Director

As I wrote in my book, *I Am Coming Sooner Than You Think*, my wife and I were called by the Lord as foreign missionaries—specifically to Pattaya, Thailand in the fall of 2010. We paid our own expenses with no organizational support. We initially went to Bangkok, Thailand as a team member for Randy Clark's Thailand Ministry Crusade to Bangkok, as we were attending his School of Supernatural Ministry in Mechanicsburg, PA.

Five months later we arrived in Pattaya, Thailand for a year of ministry. Soon after our arrival, we met Angela and immediately became fast friends. On the occasions we went with her to minister to the families in the slums, we were impressed with her love and concern for the people and her willingness to help them in their need. The children loved the Bible teachings, games, and the love she so willingly poured into them.

One miracle He did not perform for us was learning the Thai language. We tried our best, but our instructor finally gave up on us. We just could not master the total aspect of the language. When I read about Angela's struggle with learning the Thai language in her book, I could empathize with her. In her case, however, she did not give up and allowed the Lord to teach her perseverance in the process. In our case, the Lord provided an interpreter whenever we needed one. Angela was one of our answers to that prayer. Whenever we were with her in ministry, she provided the interpretation we needed.

In subsequent trips to Southeast Asia, we made short trips to Pattaya and discovered that Angela had met a Cambodian-American man name Thearith from California via the Internet and subsequently married him. It wasn't until I read Angela's book that I realized how the Lord had orchestrated such an improbable event. Her readers will be amazed!

Since then, we have remained in contact with Angela and Thearith. We have followed and supported their ministry as they were also sent to Cambodia and then to Pittsburgh, PA. We were thrilled to see God give them three beautiful children and we have prayed for Angela as she battles with the new challenge of cancer. As someone who received a godly miraculous healing from stage 4 cancer, I can identify with the struggle she is going through and believe the Lord can do for her what He did for me.

I know that as you read *Finding God's Goodness in Unexpected Places*, you will find your faith in God strengthened. You will also be challenged in your willingness to follow the Lord in whatever He calls you to do.

> Eugene Pratt, Retired Judge & District Attorney; Independent Missionaries; Author of *I Am Coming Sooner Than You Think*

Angela's book paints a beautiful picture of a God who really wants to communicate with His children. Readers will be encouraged to make space to listen to God and allow Him to participate in their lives.

> Eva and Bruce Robinson, Retired Missions Pastors & Leadership Coaches

My wife and I have known Angela for the past few years. We used to live in the same district in Phnom Penh, Cambodia, and we would fellowship often. Her family spent a few days with our family when we lived in Colorado Springs, Colorado. We believe God has called Angela to be a voice in this season in her life. Her faith story will inspire you to trust God and His calling. You will enjoy this book!

> Ken & Rachel Kong, Navigators World Missions—Missionaries in Cambodia

I'm writing this in Pattaya, Thailand, not far from the slums where Angela and Thearith faithfully served. I just finished reading the manuscript, and it deeply challenged and impacted me! Though we've never actually served on a ministry team together, we have a very real connection with this amazing couple. For the first five years that my wife Pat and I lived in Thailand, we were serving with Cambodian people in the Khao I Dang refugee camp near the Thai/Cambodian border. God used this time to connect our hearts with the Khmer people. Since then, we've been working with Thais in Bangkok, and actually did pre-marriage counseling with Thearith and Angela in the weeks before their wedding!

Reading Angela's story filled me with many thoughts and emotions. I feel gratitude and appreciation for the way she and Thearith let God use them among both Thai and Khmer people in these two nations. I feel deep respect and awe for them because of the way they have steadfastly loved, trusted, and honored God through the extreme challenges they've gone through. I feel humbled by Angela's open and vulnerable sharing of the struggles she has experienced. I also feel strong hope for the future, *regardless of what may come*, because of the beautiful picture of God's amazing character I see expressed through the pages of this book.

Angela and Thearith have traveled through some valleys that most of us cannot understand, and would certainly not choose to go through. But their story inspires confidence in me that no matter what may come, I don't need to worry because the Creator and Sustainer of the universe is with us, and will never leave us.

Sam Sarvis, Former YWAM Thailand
National Director & YWAM Indochina-
Philippines Regional Leadership Team

Sometimes circumstances in our lives test our faith to the limit, whether that be heartaches from loss or extreme physical trials. Angela Cheng has faced them all in a relatively short time, much like Job. While most of us would squirm and complain, Angela has faced her trials with her heart set on God, His word, and His promises. Her anxious thoughts and sorrows were replaced with God's peace as she held on tightly to Him. Working alongside Angela for many years in Thailand, I saw firsthand her strong faith and determination to let God guide her life on a daily basis. This book will inspire readers to trust God even in the darkest of valleys.

Lee Ann Sidebottom, Pattaya Slum
Ministries Founder, YWAM – Thailand

This is a beautiful testimony from a woman of faith. I had the privilege of getting to know Angela in Thailand and I have witnessed her going through the ups and downs of life. I have a deep respect for her godly and faithful response to so many challenges. Reading this book you will be encouraged, challenged, and inspired.

Nella Davidse, Founder of Tamar
Center in Pattaya, Thailand

Angela Cheng has written a book filled with stories of faith and God at work. Her story spans continents, trials, and deep pain, yet in it all is the grace of God. The questions at the end of each chapter help to personalize the story and encourage the reader to pause and reflect on the ways of God. Angela was sent out as a missionary from our church and over the years we have watched her hold onto God in the midst of great hardship, learning to listen to His voice and trusting His word. This book will challenge you in your faith and grow you in endurance and faith.

Mike M., Elmbrook Church Pastor
of Mission and Mobilization in
Brookfield, WI

I've had the privilege of personally knowing Angela and Thearith Cheng and I've followed their journey as a couple and as missionaries in Thailand, Cambodia, and Pittsburgh. In this book, Angela tells her own story of how God met her and called her to be a single missionary but gave her the promise of being married and the mother of three children, as she is today. It reads like she is personally talking with you as she recounts her life's experiences of walking with the Lord, the blessings and trials she has faced, and how God has proved His goodness and faithfulness to her and her family.

I recommend this book to anyone who desires to better know God and His intimate ways with us, His children.

Andy Brown, Retired Missionary &
Founding Pastor of La Vina Church,
Laguna Niguela, CA

This book is an invitation. In its pages, you are invited to walk into Angela's heart and faith. She could have written about her many, many incredible adventures on the mission field, but she doesn't. She wants you to know Jesus. That's her heart's cry, her life call—her invitation to you in this book. I've been loving and serving God in Thailand for over 30 years as part of YWAM Thailand. In these years, I have had the privilege of walking beside and with Angela. She is an amazing warrior of love for Jesus. So may I make a suggestion? Don't eat this book in one gulp. Take a bite at a time. Chew on it. Swallow deeply the truth of Jesus. From the inside out, you will be changed.

> Linda Herrmann, Former Director of
> Project L.I.F.E. Foundation and YWAM
> Thailand National Leadership Team

God's heart has always drawn Angela to the minorities, the vulnerable, those without a voice, and the poor and her answer has always been yes. As you read *Finding God's Goodness in Unexpected Places*, tears will come to your eyes, laughter will surround you, and the challenges of a missionary calling will grab your heart. God will speak to you, if you ask Him to lead and guide you.

We in YWAM-Thailand were blessed and honored to have Angela and Thearith serving amongst the poorest in Pattaya. They listened to God and they can show you what missions looks like from the inside, particularly from the amazing character of God, language and culture learning, and remembering how God has led you, step by step. They show you what a missionary family looks like and how God speaks and partners with a multi-cultural family. Angela, Thearith, Hadassa, Micah, and Zion all faced the challenges of the miscarrying of three babies Selah, Samuel, and Zoe. They have faced the challenges and impact of COVID-19 on their family and most recently, the impact of cancer upon Angela.

You will not be able to put this book down. God's provisions are wonderful. The body of Christ around the world is amazing. Come on this journey to *Finding God's Goodness in Unexpected Places* where you will find God. When you do, your life will be forever changed.

> Steve Goode. International Elder YWAM Mercy Ministries; Author of *Bring Your Eyes and See: Our Journey Into Justice, Compassion, and Action* – Bangkok, Thailand

For more than two decades, Angela has taught me to see beauty and God's goodness in the faces of neglected children and to feel God's love living through the tough moments of human existence. It is one thing to talk about faith and spirituality. It is much harder to live through painful experiences to feel God's love and be authentic to His mission for us. Her stories, insights, and life continue to inspire me to live a more authentic life and be closer to God's goodness.

> Hung Nguyen. Executive Director Emeritus at the Richard Mauthe Center for Faith, Spirituality, and Social Justice –Green Bay, WI

Angela's story is powerful evidence that God knows the deepest desires of our hearts and

can answer our prayers in surprising, wonderful, miraculous ways—leaving us in awe of who
He is and what He can do. I trust that you will
be deeply touched and inspired by Angela's experiences and reflections of the faithfulness of
our heavenly Father, who loves us and cares for
us in awesome ways, even and especially in the
most difficult moments of loss and trauma in life.
I love the unique and wonderful way each chapter ends with very powerful and thought-pro-
voking reflection questions that guide us in rec-
ognizing God's goodness and compassion in our
lives, which makes this book stand out among
other autobiographies. By God's grace, my story and insight helped encourage Angela on her
health journey, but Angela's experiences and
testimony as a young adult woman who sought
the Lord and found hope and joy in Him ministered to my heart; I had some good cries while
reading this book!

> Bailey O'Brien, stage 4 melanoma
>   survivor, cancer coach, and founder
>   of Momentum, a cancer practitioner
>   group

Encountering God's love in painful times
is a necessary part of any believer's life. *Finding
God's Goodness in Unexpected Places* brings
the reader through Angela's journey of walking
in intimacy with God through life's hardships.
For the past 20 years, she has served the Lord
in missions, discovering God's joy and blessings through it all. Their story of *Finding God's
Goodness in Unexpected Places* shows the fulfillment of the promises of God found in Isaiah
45:3: "I will give you the treasures of darkness

and hidden riches of secret places, that you may know that I, the Lord, who call you by your name, am the God of Israel."

Mark Cornacchione, YWAM Pittsburgh Base Director

Finding
God's
Goodness
in

UNEXPECTED
PLACES

ANGELA CHENG

urbanpress

Pittsburgh, Pennsylvania
USA

Finding God's Goodness in Unexpected Places
by Angela Cheng
Copyright ©2023 Angela Cheng

ISBN 978-1-63360-212-0

For Worldwide Distribution
Printed in the USA

Urban Press
P.O. Box 8881
Pittsburgh, PA 15221-0881
412.646.2780

BOOK PROCEEDS
AN INVITATION TO YOU

BOOK PROCEEDS

All proceeds from book sales will be given to
global missions work,
including sponsoring national missionaries and
their ministries.

AN INVITATION FROM ME TO YOU

The idea for this book was birthed over the past year while I was walking through a deep valley and found myself in many unexpected places. Those unexpected places included surgery tables, ICU rooms, ER visits, deep grief and loss associated with transitioning from one country to another, trauma, and an intense healing regime while recovering my life spiritually, physically, and emotionally. It's been the hardest year and the richest year, which seems paradoxical.

It was rich and rewarding even though I was walking through trial after trial. Rich in the sense that I saw the goodness of God in His presence, rich while walking in His peace, rich from His provision, and rich because I anchored myself in His promises. During this year, I often cried out to God in thanksgiving for His goodness. The events caused me to look back and share with you God's goodness in my story that's taken me to many places and nations—all of the unexpected. The one thing I came to expect, however, was God's faithfulness through it all. Thus I have chosen *Finding God's Goodness in Unexpected Places* as the title.

Life is full of the unexpected: unexpected blessings, unexpected tragedies, unexpected gains and losses. It's easy to see God in the good but how about the hard, the ugly, and the waiting? My hope is that as you read these stories, they will cause you to find the fingerprints of God's goodness in your own story. May reading this inspire your faith journey and encourage you to believe and see God do what may appear to be impossible—to show Himself strong in your own unexpected places of testing and trial. That's my prayer for you.

I have included at the end of each chapter a few questions you can use for self-reflection followed by a prayer. You may even want to use the book and then those questions for family or small group study. However you choose to use them, my hope is that as you read and reflect, you will taste and see the Lord's goodness and realize the truth of what Paul wrote:

> What, then, shall we say in response to these things? If God is for us, who can be against us? He who did not spare his own Son, but gave him up for us all— how will he not also, along with him, graciously give us all things? Who will bring any charge against those whom God has chosen? It is God who justifies. Who then is the one who condemns? No one. Christ Jesus who died—more than that, who was raised to life—is at the right hand of God and is also interceding for us. Who shall separate us from the love of Christ? Shall trouble or hardship or persecution or famine or nakedness or danger or sword? As it is written: "For your sake we face death all day long; we are considered as sheep to be slaughtered."

No, in all these things we are more than conquerors through him who loved us. For I am convinced that neither death nor life, neither angels nor demons, neither the present nor the future, nor any powers, neither height nor depth, nor anything else in all creation, will be able to separate us from the love of God that is in Christ Jesus our Lord (Romans 8:31-39).

Angela Cheng
Pittsburgh, PA USA
February 2023

1

FROM A WISCONSIN FARM TO THE NATIONS

Keep trusting in the Lord and do what
is right in His eyes. Fix your heart on
the promises of God, and you will dwell
in the land, feasting on His faithfulness.
Find your delight and true pleasure in
Yahweh, and He will give you what you
desire most. Give God the right to direct
your life, and as you trust Him along the
way, you'll find He pulled it off perfectly
(Psalm 37:3-5, TPT).

I grew up a farmer's daughter on a fami-
ly-owned dairy farm in Wisconsin. I have sweet
memories of many activities that shaped my
childhood: helping Dad milk the cows, picking
big rocks out of the farm fields in spring before
planting season, years of small town high school
sports, and celebrating birthdays and holidays
with extended family living close by.

Where I grew up, everyone in our small
town of 1,000 knew everyone else. I wasn't
aware of fear associated with evil and crimes,
nor did I see much cultural diversity. My parents paid the extra to have my three younger

siblings and I attend private Catholic school where we started our school day by attending a daily Mass. I am grateful my parents instilled in us an awareness of our Creator God and the importance of being part of a faith community.

I was excited to spread my wings after high school to learn and have adventures at college. My favorite undergraduate class was Minority Groups. I learned for the first time about diverse people groups, refugees, and the world of minorities. Through that class, I met my first cross-cultural friend who founded a project for the Hmong refugee population that immigrated from Southeast Asia. God was planting a seed in me for that part of the world before I even knew it. I volunteered at my friend's refugee project throughout my college years.

Upon leaving my parent's home for college, another new aspect of college was binge drinking and partying through the weekends. I also stopped going to church.

My first job out of college was in media marketing, and I was living the dream. All appeared well with me on the outside. I had a business job traveling to exotic destinations while wining and dining clients. I was working up the corporate ladder while pursuing my Masters, and had a serious boyfriend with a potential marriage on the horizon.

But on the inside, I was unfulfilled, had no peace, and felt dissatisfied. I like to say that I had a Solomon experience . . . in the book of his sayings named Ecclesiastes. Solomon was the wisest man who ever lived except for Christ. He composed the book of Ecclesiastes to examine and lament how meaningless human effort and toil are apart from God—along with the accumulation of stuff that leaves people unfulfilled. "Yet when I surveyed all that my hands had done and what I had toiled to achieve, everything was meaningless, a chasing after the wind; nothing was gained under the sun" (Ecclesiastes 2:11). Not having Christ in my life left me feeling purposeless, even though I was in fancy places with important people on numerous business trips.

At the same time, what my parents instilled in us kept nagging me: money cannot bring anyone happiness. I knew there must be more to life than the American dream of buying a home with a white picket fence and having 2.2 kids. This so-called happily-ever-after story didn't seem that happy or worthy of the effort I was investing in it. I began to reflect on questions like, *What's my purpose on earth? Accumulating things and experiences? Where is God in this? What does He think of this? What does He want from me?*

I came to agree with Solomon that stuff can't bring inner peace or joy. *So what does?* During that time, God put a number of Christian witnesses in my life, including my brother and his missionary friends and some Christian business clients. I saw something radically different with these people. A business client and I had enlightening faith conversations in Mexico that sparked an interest in me to find a vibrant church where I could learn and grow. Though I had not attended church consistently for a number of years, a church course called "Becoming a Contagious Christian" helped me understand what Christ did for me on the cross. I prayed asking Jesus to be the Lord of my life and personal Savior.

Church then became more than just something I checked off my Sunday to do list. I was entering into a relationship with God made possible through Christ. We were always intended to walk closely with God like Adam did in the Garden, until sin separated us. I had invited Jesus to take the wheel and be the driver of my car—my life. I made that commitment and I have not looked back, pursuing Him first and foremost in all things.

Eight months after making that decision, I resigned from my business job to attend a Bible-based discipleship training school with Youth With A Mission (YWAM), and I've been involved in ministry and missions since then. That was in 2003. I can say Almighty God—three in one, the Father, Son, and Holy Spirit—has been my leader and anchor. He has seen me through many adventures, taking me to 35 nations, including 15 years living as a Christian missionary in Southeast Asia. I ended up lived a good chunk of my life in developing and Third World countries, got married and had kids later in life, and now consider numerous places my home.

I was quite shy as a child but when God got hold in my life, I became a new person! Courage and stepping out in faith on the path less traveled replaced the timidity I had grown up with. I no longer had the desire to live the American dream. When I started to write this book, I was reminded that as a little girl I had sent in my opinion to the city newspaper and the paper published it. In it, I questioned why the media only seemed to share the bad news instead of more good news.

That has now become the essence of this book: to testify of the goodness of God in the unexpected places He has led a simple, quiet gal like me. May this book encourage you to see God's goodness in the unexpected places you find yourself as I have learned to do.

REFLECTIVE QUESTIONS

1. Where do you see God at work behind the scenes in your formative years? How have those experiences shaped your faith story?

2. What was an area of your personality that was unleashed when God took control of your life?

3. My life passage is,

> "Keep trusting in the Lord and do what is right in His eyes. Fix your heart on the promises of God, and you will dwell in the land, feasting on His faithfulness. Find your delight and true pleasure in Yahweh, and He will give you what you desire most. Give God the right to direct your life, and as you trust Him along the way, you'll find He pulled it off perfectly" (Psalm 37:3-5, TPT).

The Lord didn't create us because He was lonely or needed workers for His kingdom, but created us so He could delight and take pleasure in us and we in Him. What does delighting in the Lord and Him delighting in you look like?

Thank You, Lord, that You created me out of delight, out of desire to have a relationship with me. Thank You for the people and experiences that have drawn me closer to You. Thank You, Lord, for Your word that is never changing and promises that You will never leave us or forsake us.

2

PICKING OUT LICE ON A COLOMBIAN ISLAND

> The fundamental fact of existence is that
> this trust in God, this faith, is the firm
> foundation under everything that makes
> life worth living. It's our handle on what
> we can't see (Hebrews 11:1, MSG).

In previous years, I was living it up at five star hotels in the Caribbean with my marketing job. Now there I was on an extremely poor island in Colombia for a month, picking out lice in kids' hair. It was a summer of sleeping on wooden church pews, legs filled with too-many-to-count mosquito bites, no air conditioning, no running water, and limited electricity. How did I end up at this unexpected place?

It was my first mission trip seeing poverty face to face. It was there that the Lord changed my heart and shaped my future. I saw a joy and contentment in the faces of believers who had so little but found all they needed in Christ. I confronted my bad attitudes due to the hot, humid weather while trying not to scratch the zillion bug bumps that covered my legs.

About six months prior, I had invited Jesus to be my Lord and Savior. I experienced Him as the Lover of my soul, one who knows me intimately and loves me in a way that no human can. He knows my thoughts from afar before I even speak them, knows when I lay down and when I rise, *and* knows every hair on my head. I had an inner peace never experienced before that is only found in Christ—a peace that would see me through many future storms in life. I had a strong desire to read His Word and now it made sense. I wanted to know God more.

The idea came to me of taking time off to grow as a lover and disciple of Christ. We only live once, right? Let's live it to its fullest. So I took the risk, stepped out in faith, and resigned from my plush media-marketing job. As I completed my half-year Christian Discipleship Training School (DTS) run by one of the world's largest Christian missions organizations, Youth With A Mission (YWAM), I didn't know if I would return to my business job or if God had something else in mind.

I do want to speak a word of caution that not everyone needs to follow my example. You don't need to stop all that you're doing to know God more intimately! Each of our journeys is different and how God leads each of us is unique. Discipleship training is what I felt compelled to do and it was my first big stepping out in my journey with God. I had saved a chunk of money for a down payment on a house, but instead I used it to pay for the discipleship course.

The course was three months of weekly lectures on topics like hearing the voice of God, the Father heart of God, understanding the Bible, inner healing, missions, etc. My lecture phase was followed by a two-month mission trip to apply what I had learned in the classroom. This invaluable training changed the trajectory of my life's course.

On my first mission trip, I went to Colombia on the course's mission trip phase. That summer, I struggled. I wasn't the one on mission team saying, "Oh, I love this and want to do this for the rest of my life!" Neither was I exuding tons of joy being there. I kept my struggles to myself and remained quiet, bringing to the Lord my struggles with the heat, poverty, and my own selfishness. It was difficult and humbling.

Who would have thought years later that I would be leading and loving a ministry reaching out to kids in poverty-stricken areas, regularly combing out lice, and pulling out simple mats in their communities for play fun at Christ-centered kids' clubs in Asia. As I welcomed many mission teams like the one I was on in Colombia, I always wanted to connect with the one on the team who was struggling because that had been me not so many years before.

During that difficult time in Colombia, I asked God if He wanted to me go back to the business world to shine His light as a "marketer of the Gospel?" I also asked if He had a specific people group or nation He wanted me to serve. Every week during our course, we had prayed for various nations. One week we watched a short video about child trafficking in Thailand and prayed for that nation.

As we prayed, I felt God's still small voice in my heart saying, "I'm calling you to go there to bring healing to the children in My name." I knew in my heart it wasn't a short time commitment and that my call wasn't just to Thailand but

to all of Southeast Asia. One leader felt prompt-
ed to get up on stage during the prayer time and
say that God was calling some in the room to
go to these places as missionaries. I knew I was
one of them.

After the discipleship training course was
finished, I went back to Wisconsin. I served
two years in urban youth missions while preparing to move to Southeast Asia. The Lord is
the perfect gentleman in that as I invited Him
to lead me, He opened the right doors, conversations, and counsel to make it happen. Those
God-ordained connections gave me the courage
to move halfway around the world to a foreign
land where I didn't know anyone.

My home church rallied around me in
prayer and supported my going on a month-
long trip to connect with YWAM and other
missionaries they knew there. Though I came
back with more questions than answers, I knew
God was putting it on my heart to serve at-risk
children. I also knew that YWAM was the right
missions organization for me to join, and that I
was indeed making a long-term commitment.
My days in the world of business were over and
my entre into God's world of missions was here.

REFLECTIVE QUESTIONS

1. Was there a time when you saw God turn a struggle you were having into something good and beautiful? His promise in Romans 8:28 is that God works all things for the good of those who love Him and are called according to His purposes. Thank Him for turning ashes into beauty, sorrow into joy. Only He can do that.

2. If you were on an island like I was with limited resources and no Wi-Fi or online shopping, what do you think would comfort you and see you through? What does your answer say about what your heart treasures? "For where your treasure is, there your heart will also be" (Matthew 6:21).

Lord, You are the same, yesterday, today and forever. You are the firmest foundation that I can build my life upon. Give me the courage to step out of the comforts of my life to share Your love and what You have done in my life with those around me. Father, is there a people group You want to send me to, have me be involved in? Here I am, Lord. Reveal who You want me to show Your love and kindness to—whether they are nearby or across the oceans.

3

CLIMBING STAIRS IN BANGKOK

"When Yahweh delights in how you
live your life, he establishes your every
step. If they stumble badly they will still
survive, for the Lord lifts them up with
his hands" (Psalm 37:23-24, TPT).

I was climbing up the long flights of stairs of our mission center in the crazy tropical heat of Bangkok when the Lord gave me a revelation in an unexpected place. I was headed to our staff meeting after a morning of sitting in language class, barely uttering baby sounds of the Thai tonal language. How in the world was I ever going to speak this language? In my first year, I had committed to full-time language learning with the dream of being able to communicate God's love to the people to whom He called me.

My days consisted of riding the city bus an hour to language class, with windows wide-open, taking in the pollution, smells, heat, and noise of the bustling city. This lover of quiet, wide-open spaces was being tested in more ways than I desired. Then I sat in a three-hour language class trying to learn a complicated foreign language before another hour-long bus ride back to the center where I finished the day with two hours of language homework. I was frustrated with the process of trying to learn the characters and remember each sound.

As I approached the middle of my first year in Thailand, my language-learning classroom was becoming a jail cell. Was I ever going to speak, read, and write this language? Thai language has 72 characters, split into 44 consonants, 28 vowels, and five tones. Say a tone wrong and you could end up offending someone—which I did many times! On top of that, Thai has no spacing in between words like English does, so I become like a child, learning sounds and memorizing word combinations with a lot of sweat, time, and tears. But let me get back to my revelation.

That day as I ascended those stairs, the Lord impressed upon me that I wanted to be at the top of the staircase as quickly as possible, just like I wanted to learn Thai. However, I needed to take it step by step in my classes just like that staircase. Since language learning is a process of taking small steps and if I kept taking the next one and then the next one, I would eventually get there. More or less I felt Him saying to trust the process and the journey on my way to the destination.

I had so fixed my eyes on the end goal that I ignored the process and got frustrated, thinking I would never get there! The Lord was saying, "Just be in the day, in the now, and I will get you to your destination." And that is exactly what happened. Years later I found myself translating speech from Thai to English at meetings and big events, leading a ministry completely in Thai language, while also reading and leading Bible studies in my new language. My favorite activity was (and still is) worshiping God with Thai people in their native tongue. It took time, energy, and grit, but it happened by the grace of God for His glory.

REFLECTIVE QUESTIONS

1. What is the God-sized dream in your heart that seems impossible and requires more than you can wrap your heart and mind around?

2. What is the next small step you can take to move yourself forward toward that dream? Do your part and watch what God will do with that.

Father, I know with You nothing is impossible! All things are possible in You. I'm stepping out in faith toward the dream and desire You placed on my heart; I won't give up, even though I struggle to get there. I will anchor myself in Your word and Your promises. Give me the courage to do and keep doing what seems impossible. Give me patience and grit to continue in the process when the end seems so far away. May others see You in me through the journey!

4

A THAILAND BEACH VISION AND EHARMONY

"Waiting on God in this way is true
faith—no agenda of one's own, no
deadlines, no demands on what God must
do. Simply an open heart and open hands
to receive that which God shall choose
and a perfect confidence that what He
chooses will be better than our best"
(*The Path of Loneliness* by
Elizabeth Elliott).

"Yet I am confident I will see the Lord's
goodness while I am here in the land of
the living. Wait patiently for the Lord.
Be brave and courageous. Yes, wait
patiently for the Lord"
(Psalm 27:13-14, NLT).

Ever since I was a little girl, I dreamt of
being married and having children. In sixth
grade for career 'dress up' day at school, I chose
to dress up as a mother with a red farmer's
handkerchief in my hair, a grey floral kitchen
apron, and carrying my Cabbage Patch doll
while classmates dressed as lawyers, business

people, and the like. I thought being a mother would be a wonderful career. I realized years later that God placed that vocation in me to nurture, love, and care for children. It was a part of my DNA. The most important work I will ever do is within the walls of my home, cherishing the people who come into my life for me to love.

Fast forward through dating and boyfriends to age 25 when the trajectory of my life changed. I chose Jesus to be the Lord of my life, which meant surrendering to Him and trusting His rock-solid character. I yielded my dreams, desires, and ambitions to Him—choosing to follow His prompts and leadership. One of the 'rights' I surrendered to Him was the right to be married, understanding that true joy, contentment, and peace in my life would only come through letting Him choose what is best—whether married or single, rich or poor. I repented of the times I had strayed into impurity in relationships and chose from that point on to try my best to purify my thoughts and actions.

During my first year in Thailand, I felt lonely and isolated. I struggled with hopelessness, questioning God's goodness, and with restlessness in my singleness. Was I going to be single the rest of life? Would I be okay with that? Would I have joy and let His beauty shine through me even if I am an older single missionary woman? Or will I wallow in self-pity? I worked through those questions both with God and also sharing with others. He put radiant, faith-filled single woman across my path who inspired me to believe that if singleness was a part of the plan, I was going to be a joy-filled beautiful bride of Christ shining His light into my old age.

My first Christmas in Thailand was difficult. It was my first major holiday away from my family while I was living across the world, feeling lonely without any plans for the week off. The foreign families were all with their loved ones and a lot of national staff went back to their villages. At the last minute, I decided to go away to a beach town a couple hours south.

One particular morning on the beach I had an unexpected surprise. I had been journaling and reading the Word when I glanced up to see a taller white woman with a shorter Asian man walking the shore with three Asian children. I felt the Spirit tell me to write down what I saw because it was important. I did and circled it numerous times. I wondered if that could be a picture of my future.

Maybe what I saw was a foreign missionary working at a children's home while mothering boys and girls. Maybe that would be the next step after language learning. God did indeed open up motherhood opportunities for me serving as a spiritual mother to many slum and street kids in the ministry I joined after language learning. For eight years, I served and then led a Thai team of Jesus lovers who would go into slum communities to share the love of Christ to children and families. The Lord was gracious to give me a future picture of what He had for me.

Yet my heart's deep desire was to have a family of my own. God never answered the question of whether I would get married or not, but He did tell me to trust Him. I especially clung to Psalm 84:11: "No good thing will He withhold to those that fear Him" and to Psalm 37:3-7, which became my life verses:

"Trust in the Lord and do good; dwell

in the land and enjoy safe pasture. Take delight in the Lord, and he will give you the desires of your heart. Commit your way to the Lord; trust in him and he will do this: He will make your righteous reward shine like the dawn, your vindication like the noonday sun. Be still before the Lord and wait patiently for him; do not fret when people succeed in their ways, when they carry out their wicked schemes."

A couple of years after I had that beach vision, I was back in the States to be part of the wedding of a close friend. I had gone to a prayer chapel for an afternoon to seek the Lord when He asked me what I was looking for in a husband. That was the first time I heard God speak to me about a life partner. I told God four things that I desired in a man and wrote them down: a man who loves the Lord, a man of missions, a man to whom I would be attracted to physically, emotionally, and spiritually (and him to me); and a shared enjoyment of hobbies and interests.

In the few weeks following that chapel conversation, three different people from three different places spoke a word about God bringing a husband into my life. They told me he would be a missionary man and that God was first going to grow me in the Spirit and Word to prepare me for marriage and ministry before bringing my husband to me. God was going to do it—bring us together. The 'words' were very specific and people said things that echoed what I had told God I desired in a life partner that day in the prayer chapel.

Actually a week or so after that time in

a chapel, I was in Toronto at a church when I fell to my knees in worship while having an encounter with the Lord. I don't know how long I was down, but He told me that I would be married and have three children. He even revealed to me the gender of each child. When I rose to visit the restroom, a pastor from Holland who was walking through stopped me and asked to pray for me.

He spoke out that I would have three kids, also describing the gender of each child. It was exactly what the Lord had just showed me when I was laying in His presence. It was a little crazy for me not knowing where I was to go from there, but I knew I was going to get married and have three kids. Never mind the fact that there was no potential man on the horizon, especially the city where I was ministering. My Father was giving me a promise to hold on to. The Lord loves to give His children hope and promises.

From that point on, my prayers changed from surrendering to singleness to praying with confidence that my life partner was somewhere out there. I love, love, love the meaning of faith found in Hebrews 11:1: "Faith is confidence in what we hope for and assurance about what we do not see." Faith is rooted in a person—God, who does not lie, keeps His promises, and is the same yesterday, today and forever. He would bring my life partner to me in His time, in His way, and for His glory. When contending for a promise from God, we have a choice as to the thoughts we will think concerning that promise. Will they be influenced by circumstances, or will they stay anchored in the Word and what He has spoken?

What God spoke happened two years later.

I had just finished a few days of fasting to pray and seek the Lord at our YWAM training center. One of my leaders and his wife felt they had a word from God for me. They encouraged me to stay in contact with anyone who God brought into my life who was part of a visiting team or in Thailand. They also said if I was interested in him, I should stay in contact with him through emails or whatever means possible. They also said God values family more than ministry, and if getting to know someone meant not giving 100% to ministry work for a season, I should be okay with that if having a family was what I desired.

I was grateful but there was still no one on my horizon. Seven days later, I was matched with my husband on eHarmony and his picture and profile caught my attention. He looked attractive and appeared that he had a passion for God and children's ministry. After that, I messaged him and we started to communicate through emails and then video calls for the next six months—getting to know each other's heart, vision, and passions.

I felt God saying, "Open your heart, daughter, and get to know him as a friend." God not only gave me dreams about this man but also provided confirmation from a dear friend in another part of the world who randomly messaged me that she had a dream I was getting engaged to be married. Nothing like that had ever happened to me before. It encouraged me greatly, especially because I was in Thailand and he was in California. God gave me further confirmation as I got to know him more and more through our long distance conversations. What was interesting about all this was that we still hadn't met in person.

The gentleman's name is Thearith, and 18 months later he became my husband and my love. He is Cambodian-American and happens to be a bit shorter than me! Isn't God amazing in his care and level of detail in our lives? When I was at a low and lonely point a few years earlier, God gave me a picture of my future while on the beach: a taller white woman walking with a shorter Asian man with three kids by their side.

Thearith was born in Cambodia, which borders Thailand. His family was sponsored to move to America when he was five years old and the Khmer Rouge genocide had taken place in his home country. When I met him, he was working at the local YMCA with children, serving at his local church in the children's ministry, and had started an outreach to refugees with a few Khmer buddies. They would set out mats in the local park for refugee kids to come and learn about God. We were both rolling out mats in different parts of the world for the children to come and receive.

His heart's desire was to go back to his homeland to serve the poor, especially children. He had told God he would go when God brought the wife who had a heart for the nations into his life. Obviously much of what we were learning about each other was a perfect match—our passions, our walk with Jesus, and vocation. We enjoyed getting to know each other and were excited to finally meet each other in person.

When I was back in the States after six months of conversing with him online, I flew out to meet him and stayed with my aunt. It is much like what God did with me when calling me to Thailand. I had never been to Thailand, yet God was giving me a love for the people and their country before I had ever met them. Then, the more I prayed, the more certain I was God was calling me to Southeast Asia. Now the same thing was happening with Thearith in the same way. The more I prayed about our relationship, the more peace I had. I knew in my spirit when I flew out to meet him for the first time that this was the man God had for me.

We flew back and forth between California and Wisconsin to meet each other's family, church families, and spend time together over the next several months. Then he took a faith trip to see me and the ministry I led in Thailand. I refer to it as a faith trip because he didn't have the money to come visit me. On top of that, his car had died on the freeway the month before he planned to visit. After that someone in his church felt led to give Thearith a car he no longer need. Individuals from his church then also gave him money to go to Thailand! It was Thearith's first taste of trusting God for finances with entering into full-time missionary service.

When he got back to California, the pastoral staff informed him that a prophetic minister had visited and asked if there was a Thearith in their church. He couldn't pronounce the name but wrote out Thearith's name on paper. When he was informed there was, he went on to say that this Thearith would be used by God to gather the children to worship in Asia. That was a significant confirmation for Thearith upon returning from Thailand that marrying me and moving overseas was a part of God's plan for his life.

He stepped out in faith again by coming back a couple months later to do our mission organization training course in Bangkok. It was a huge step of faith for him since he was leaving his family, his job, and his life as he knew it to move overseas for a gal, to follow God, and to see the dream he had prayed for come to fruition.

During that time, we saw each other on the weekends and started pre-marital counseling. After he got back from a missions trip to China with his DTS, he proposed to me in Thailand. I planned our wedding at my home church in Wisconsin while overseas. By faith, I bought a $99 wedding dress online that I tried on two weeks before our wedding and saw an amazing team from church put together a beautiful celebration of two lives coming together to love and serve our Lord.

I got my money's worth with the dress because I ended wearing it four times. Besides our wedding at our home church, my parents hosted a reception in the town where I grew up, his mother hosted a Cambodian reception in California, and we had a garden reception among our YWAM family in Thailand. To top it all off, we honeymooned in Hawaii. It was a dream come true to experience the goodness of God after many years of waiting and believing God.

REFLECTIVE QUESTIONS

1. What is a desire of your heart for which you have been praying and waiting? To wait means to have confident expectation in the Lord. In the process of waiting, we hold onto the person of hope, the Lord.

2. What has surrendering to the Lord looked like in your life?

3. What has He used or what is He using as a symbol of hope while you wait?

Lord, Your word says that those who hope in You will not be disappointed (Isaiah 49:23). I open my heart and hands to receive what You have for me. Lord, You are a better choice. You know me better than I know myself. I trust You. I hope in You alone with all of my desires and dreams.

5

NEW NAMES IN NEW LANDS

"You will be called by a new name
that the mouth of the Lord will bestow"
(Isaiah 62:2b).

"And on the white stone is written a new
name that no knows but the one who
receives it" (Revelation 2:17).

"See what great love the Father has
lavished on us, that we should be called
children of God" (1 John 3:1).

Names have meaning because they reveal identity. Our first names are given to us by our parents and our last names often express our cultural identity. Names are also given by God and these often mark a future promise, a new beginning, a new hope, or new blessings. Often in the Old Testament, we see names given expressing what God is up to. In the New Testament, we learn that God changed Saul's name to Paul and Simon to Peter. In both cases, the change identified the new thing God was doing through them.

During my first year in Thailand, I received numerous care packages from home with angels on them. It got me thinking to the meaning of my name. Angela means *messenger of God* or *one bringing good news*. This was helpful to hold onto in times of doubt when I questioned why in the world I was struggling so much in Thailand. The reminders of my name helped fight off the negative thoughts. *God, You brought me here to share Your good news. I will learn this language. I will be able to share You in their language.*

Towards the end of my Thai language-learning phase, God gave me a new spiritual name that was prayed over me by others and it spoke of a new beginning, a new season that was coming. That name was Esther, which also happens to be my favorite book in the Bible. It's a story of a Jewish orphan girl who is chosen by the king to be the queen. Once she enters into royalty, she puts her life on the line for the sake of her people. She goes before the king without invitation to bring news that all her people were about to die unless the king reversed an evil decree. He does and God's people are spared because of Esther's courage and boldness.

This short Old Testament book makes no mention of God. Yet as I read it, I see the hand of God all over it. Isn't that like my life? If only I would open my eyes and heart to see God in my midst, I would not be so prone to discouragement and doubt. I didn't change my actual name to Esther but it certainly applied to my life because I was entering a new season of ministry by serving in the slum communities.

The Lord was giving me perspective on how He saw it—and me. My life resembled that

of Esther in that God was calling me into a roy-
al, noble calling of laying down my life for others. Nobility and royalty were attached to her
name as queen and are attached to my name as
a daughter of the King. The Lord wanted me to
embrace that as my new identity. I would be the
representative of the love of God to the abused,
downtrodden, and overlooked people living in
shacks and under trees in slum communities.
They did not choose their circumstances but hard
knocks of life had taken their toll on them. No
one saw them, but God had heard their cries and
was sending His children to them, children like
me to represent our God of love and redemption.

Those who I would help were garbage col-
lectors, former go-go bar workers, orphans, and
migrant workers. God was calling me, like He
did Esther, for such a time as this to go with boldness and courage—to go down dirt paths sometimes lined with barking slum dogs, over stinky
river canals, and into crude shacks to be a representative of perfect love. Satan, the father of lies,
often would want me to think negative thoughts:
*Nothing is changing, it was a waste of time, you
could be doing better things*. Before I even started, the Father wanted to affirm me concerning
how He saw what I was about to do. Each of us
has nobility and royalty as we live as sons and
daughters of the Most High King. God gave me a
new name at an unexpected time: Esther.

When Thearith and I were dating, we
talked about how we were marrying each other's lands so to speak. He was saying yes to me
and yes to a new land, Thailand, where I was
planted. I was saying yes to him and to a new
land, Cambodia. Thearith had shared his God
dream of going to his homeland to serve and

by marrying him, I was saying yes to moving to Cambodia when the Lord opened that door. I had been to Cambodia several times for ministry and had known in my spirit that it wasn't just Thailand, but the region of Southeast Asia to which the Lord was directing me.

The month before we got married, we were in Thailand and took a trip to visit his extended family in Cambodia. God gave me a glimpse of our future and gave us spiritual names as a couple on that trip. As the plane was descending into the rustic capital city of Phnom Penh, the Lord spoke to my heart that this would be the next land in which we would live. We went to visit a large local church to which Thearith had a connection. I was the only foreign girl in a lively church of Asians where believers were dancing, rejoicing, and worshiping in God's presence. Toward the end of service, the pastor called us out to the front and started praying that we were like Abraham and Sarah, a father and mother of nations.

A couple of days later, Thearith's buddy, who wasn't in that church service, took us to the airport. He prayed almost the identical thing that we wouldn't just be in Thailand and Cambodia, but rather from people group to people group. He prayed that we were like Abraham and Sarah in the nations—a father and mother. There would be different places in different seasons where the Lord would lead us.

This confirmed to us what we already felt in our spirits that we wouldn't just be in Thailand, but Cambodia and other places would be in our future. The Lord in His kindness confirmed these to us *before* our marriage. Oh how we need those words from the Lord, for when the fiery trials, the doubt, and the hardships come, we can then stand on the Lord's word. *Lord, You called us here and You will get us through this.*

Thearith joined the Thai team I was leading and began a ministry of serving Cambodians living in migrant worker camps in our city. As I interacted with Cambodian migrant families, God gave me a compassion for the people, like He did for the Thai people. Five years after marriage and serving the poor, God raised up a wise, mature Thai lover of God to lead the ministry I had led. This released us to move with our 2.5 year old and newborn to Cambodia.

Speaking of names, the name above all that has endeared itself to me is being called the beloved child of God. More than 20 years ago, I received that new name—a name that brings tears to my eyes when I reflect on it. It's healing balm to my weary soul, inner confidence in my steps. It's the name that all those who invite Jesus to be their Lord and Savior receive.

You see, He's the world's best gift available to those who receive Him and open it. And when we receive the gift of Christ in our lives, He gives us a new name. We are called His child, His beloved. We become sons and daughters of the King of kings and the Lord of lords. We have our identity as a child of our heavenly Father. There's no better word from God to hear than, "You are My child with whom I am well pleased. I love you. You are my daughter, you are my son."

REFLECTIVE QUESTIONS

1. What's the meaning of your name? How does it hold significance to you?

2. If the Lord gave you a new name for the season of life you are in, what would it be? Ask Him.

3. Put this book and your phone down. Be still for one minute. Ask God to speak to your heart. Do you hear Him? "I love you. You are my child." If not, then consider this promise for you found in Galatians 4:5-7:

> "To redeem those under the law, that we might receive adoption to sonship. Because you are his sons, God sent the Spirit of his Son into our hearts, the Spirit who calls out, '*Abba*, Father.' So you are no longer a slave, but God's child; and since you are his child, God has made you also an heir."

Creator of heaven and earth, Almighty Father, I adore You, the only one and true living God. God of Hope, Author of Love, You know when I sit and when I stand. You know my thoughts before I speak them. You remind me that I don't need to earn Your love. You love me in my weakest and greatest moments. I stand in awe of who You are—faithful and true. My heart is filled with gratitude that You call me Your beloved, Your child. I am royalty, a child of the King of kings and Lord of lords.

6

TWO CHILDREN

"God can do anything, you know—far
more than you could ever imagine or
guess or request in your wildest dreams!
He does it not by pushing us around but
by working within us, his Spirit deeply
and gently within us"
(Ephesians 3:20, MSG).

One of the greatest joys of my life was experiencing life growing in me, then birthing new life and being a mother to my children. One aspect of mothering I was dreading was the idea of giving birth. Maybe it's because I didn't think I could handle the pain. Or maybe it's how laboring has been portrayed in shows and movies that painted a negative picture in my mind. In the nine months leading up to the birth of our firstborn, my perspective changed dramatically as I met with my doula, prayed for supernatural birthing experience without complications, and read a book called *Supernatural Childbirth*.

I had composed prayer declarations over the pregnancy and laboring, as well as claiming peace, not fear. Once fear and the sense of being out of control set in, our bodies go into panic mode. God created our bodies to birth babies and we can do it naturally. This pain around child birthing is a healthy pain, a pain we want as hormones are released to aid in the process. And armed with that knowledge, I had one of the most exhilarating experiences of birthing a child!

FIRSTBORN: HADASSA SOVANNARY CHENG
DECEMBER 2013

My pregnancy was going well until the start of the ninth month. During a prenatal appointment, the doctor said I had high blood pressure and needed to be monitored. When I was, the doctor said I needed a C-section within a day or two because of borderline preeclampsia. I was devastated as I really believed that this birth was going to be what I had been claiming: without complications, full term, and that my mind, body, and soul would experience the birthing process in a natural way.

I consulted with my doctor in Bangkok, asking her to run tests on the baby and me to see if we were both okay to be monitored since performing a C-section seemed premature. There are options and it's good to get multiple medical opinions to know them *all* rather than assume what is suggested is best. We drove two hours to Bangkok where I had planned to have the baby.

The doctor administered a full ultrasound testing, which showed that the baby was fine but there were concerns with the high blood pressure. She assured me it was fine to wait. I spent three weeks on complete bed rest, eating a strict diet with limited sugar and salt, and tons of water, and stayed with my lovely friend, who just happened to live five minutes from the hospital.

Her place was a haven of rest and within the first week, I lost four pounds of water that I was retaining in my face, legs, and feet. I went every couple days for blood work and monitoring the baby and me. That got me a bit anxious, since I never knew what she would say and how we were doing. During this testing time, God's voice spoke to me so strongly through the Scriptures and these two stood out:

> "Faith is the assurance of things hoped for [natural, full-term birth without complications] and the conviction of things not yet seen" (Hebrews 11:1, I added the comment).

> "May God give you the desires of your heart and make all your plans succeed. He answers from His heavenly sanctuary" (Psalm 20:4, 6).

One morning when waiting on God, a third came to my mind. I felt God was showing me that I would have three weeks of rest before Haddie arrived. (And that's what it was!)

> "Wait on the Lord, be strong and take heart, wait on the Lord" (Psalm 27:14). (To wait is to have confident expectation on the thing you are waiting for – my comment.)

Through this testing, I could have given way to fear, anxiety, and doubt concerning my well-being and that of the baby. Instead, I believed the word of God and was also lifted up by the prayers of my friends and family. I made it to 40 weeks, full term as I had been declaring, and saw God restore my body as my blood work and tests all indicated I was getting better. However, my blood pressure was still high so the doctor said if I wanted to have a natural water birth, then I would have to labor at home as long as possible. That's because once I was admitted to the hospital with high blood pressure, they would perform interventions, like induce me or resort to a C-section.

Thearith had been driving to Bangkok on the weekends to be with me. We prayed together before we went to sleep the night before I was due. I remember him praying that I would go into labor that night or Sunday morning. I wanted the baby to come on a Sunday, as there are no Bangkok traffic jams on that day. I had heard many stories of babies being delivered in taxis and I didn't want to be one of them.

I remember praying over Thearith "the ministry of presence"—that I just wanted him to be present, not suggest going to hospital or taking pain medications, but to allow me to trust my body and ask for help when I needed it. One of the greatest services I've received and given to those in need or in crisis is the ministry of presence—just being there alongside of someone without saying anything unless they ask for it. He was awesome with it and such a huge support.

I ended up laboring in our room at the missionary guesthouse for five hours until Thearith called my doula and the doctor early Sunday morning. We got to the hospital fast and shortly after, our daughter arrived while I was laboring in the hospital birthing pool. I am amazed still that my body knew what to do. It was such a high and when she came out of the water and onto my chest, it was a surreal moment. I couldn't believe I had done this, that this precious life had been birthed through me. She was fully alert, quiet, and not crying, and as we got out of the water and onto the cot, the three of us, Daddy, Mom, and Haddie, spent the first two hours of her life on earth in quietness while she laid on me and started to feed. It was our first time of bonding as a family that I will never forget!

After we got into our hospital room and settled in, we called our immediate family in the States to share the joyful news. We didn't sleep all day or night because we were on such a high. I felt like I had conquered the world; the high of giving birth was surreal. We named her *Hadassa Sovannary Cheng*, her first name found in Esther 2:7. (Hadassah is the Esther's Jewish name, which means purity and righteousness.)

Esther's story reminds us that God considers us royalty and uses simple people to change the destiny of nations for His glory. We believe our girl will carry the same attributes and purpose. Her middle name is Sovannary and is Thearith's mother's Cambodian name. We admire the similar attributes of courage and strength that his mom displays. After living through a horrendous genocide in her native country, she immigrated to the States where she rose up in a new land with perseverance and stamina. We pray our daughter walks in the same strength of character.

SECOND-BORN: MICAH RITHY CHENG
AUGUST 2016

The year of Micah's birth was a year of transition for us from serving in Thailand; to living and traveling in the States for seven months of training, fundraising, and giving birth to Micah; followed by moving to Cambodia. Along with the transitions between three countries came a lot of unknowns regarding his birth. Where will I birth him? How will we pay the hospital bills while in the States? Will I have a dream birth like I had with Haddie? Will God provide a doula and midwife like I wanted?

I decided to take it to prayer and to search out the options, believing that God hears and will answer the desires of my heart. I'm His child and the Word says our heavenly Father meets our needs and gives us good gifts: "If you, imperfect as you are, know how to lovingly take care of your children and give them what's best, how much more ready is your heavenly Father to give wonderful gifts to those who ask him?" (Matthew 7:11, TPT).

As I prayed, peace and trust in God overcame the fear of the unknown. Once again, I experienced God's goodness in answering even the smallest of things. We felt God's grace carrying us through all the transitions! People prayed over us before we left Thailand about the transition season being filled with God's grace. What a gift it is to have God's grace and peace in transition.

My due date passed and every day after felt like a week. I had to remind myself that he was coming and that God would provide what I had been asking for. He did, even though I gave birth *a week past the due date*. I'm glad I trusted my instincts while in labor. The contractions intensified on the ride to the hospital. I found myself bracing the window and car seat while asking T to speed up and then slow down during contractions. When we were close to the hospital, my water broke and I felt the urge to push. I didn't tell T because I didn't want to freak him out, but did so anyways when I started to shout, telling him to get me to the hospital quickly! He was so excited that he missed the entrance to the hospital and had to drive around the block to find the entrance again.

When we arrived, I thought the baby was

coming out in the hospital parking lot. By then, I was trembling and felt the strong urge to push. The hospital security guards tried to get me into a wheelchair but I wasn't having it. Finally, the guard said "Ma'am, sit down, breathe, and don't push because you aren't going to deliver in the parking lot." They whisked me to the fourth floor and 25 minutes later, Micah arrived! T ran into the room just five minutes before Micah!

I had wanted a water birth but that didn't happen because I had delivered so quickly. However, I did get what I was praying for—to have a quicker labor at night and a healthy baby. We called our family and it was a sweet blessing this time to have Haddie, cousins, parents, and siblings come to the hospital to meet our new addition. His full name is Micah Rithy Cheng.

Micah is the name of a prophetic book of the Bible in the Old Testament. Both T and I love the verse found in Micah 6:8: "God has shown you, what is good. And what does the Lord require of you? To act justly and to love mercy. And to walk humbly with your God." We believe Micah will be a compassionate, joyful person who is known for justice and mercy. Rithy (pronounced *Rii-thee* and is a Cambodian name that means power). We don't think of this as physical power, but rather an inner power that helps one remain humble and persevere through life. We believe Micah will have an inner strength that comes from walking with the Lord.

REFLECTIVE QUESTIONS

1. When is a time that you have experienced or given the ministry of presence as Thearith did to me when I was laboring? Describe how it felt to have someone physically there in the chaos, in the uncertainty. It certainly was a gift to me.

2. I found standing on God's word is the best way to navigate new situations rather than worrying, prayer, or exploring options. Think of what helped you in a time of transition in your life or a time of unexpected events. Remember those tools as you walk through current and future unexpected life events.

3. If possible, ask your mom your birthing story. What was going on in her and your family's life at the time of your arrival. What were her emotions and experiences of bringing life into the world.

Thank You God for the life You have given me. It is a gift. Also, thank You that one of Your names is Immanuel, God with us. You are with me in the highs and lows of life. You are working things out in all the unexpected, concerning situations that come my way. Thank You for the people who come alongside me during the trials and life transitions to provide rest, comfort, and perspective.

7

THREE IN HEAVEN

> "Is anyone crying for help? God is
> listening, ready to rescue you. If your
> heart is broken, you'll find God right
> there; if you're kicked in the gut, He'll
> help you catch your breath"
> (Psalm 34:17-18, MSG).

As you may recall, I felt the Lord showed me while I was still single that I would be married and have three children, revealing to me the gender of each. Never then did I expect to walk through a season of grief and loss in miscarrying three children after Micah.

MISCARRIAGE #1: SELAH SANTAYA CHENG
MARCH 2018

It seems fitting to honor the life and gift that was growing inside of me. One year and a half after Micah, we found out we were pregnant and of course we were excited. We felt it was surely a fulfillment of God's promise that we were to have three children. We were set on the middle name "San-ta-ya," which means *promise* in Cambodian.

However, I started bleeding while ten weeks pregnant. My midwife said it could be normal and not to worry. One night, I started to have severe cramps with lower back pain like that which accompanies labor. I messaged a few friends in Cambodia and they suggested possibly getting an ultrasound. A dear friend came over to watch our sleeping kids while Thearith took me to the ER.

I am glad that I went when I did because the cramps intensified. When I got up out of the rickshaw at the hospital, I was a huge mess that continued for hours. I did not cry but I was in shock, trying to determine what my body was telling me. We waited for what seemed like forever to get an ultrasound, and it confirmed that there was no heartbeat. The baby was only measuring development of four weeks and two days.

The ER doctor was pretty firm on putting me to sleep and doing a D&C from the moment we arrived. After having been to the hospital a few times, I've learned to advocate for myself. I went through my list of questions that I ask for medical issues, which doctors there are not used to hearing. Then we made the best possible decision in the midst of the ambiguity. We trusted our intuition, signed a release, and I went home where I wanted to be.

I was a bit scared as I didn't know where my body was in the process. I leaned on Thearith, who was steady and calm, and a rock for me. When I got home, I laid on our bed and tried to sleep, I felt the Holy Spirit speak to my heart to rest and that He was with me with Thearith right by my side. Those were comforting, kind words of reassurance from my Father in the midst of a miscarriage.

The next morning, I scheduled a second opinion with another clinic in which I had more trust. It confirmed that the baby had passed. After the shock, we took time to grieve, talk, and pray together as a couple, and to process it with Haddie. We bought flowers as a family to honor the life that had been in me but had transitioned to heaven.

I saw God's love in family and friends— prayers, friends bringing over meals, people watching our children during doctor appointments, and the giving of flowers. I saw God's hand from several doctors and midwives' friends who gave me counsel as I walked through the miscarriage. And, I saw God through my husband—by his care, love, and embrace. We are loved and oh, what a gift that is during a difficult time. As I journaled what I felt, I wrote:

> *A desire and a dream of ours – lost, broken, no longer happening right now. Sad and grieving the loss. No longer there. Hard to swallow the reality. In the midst of that I hold onto as my anchor, God's goodness. I trust in His character. I trust in His best for my family and me. All I need I find in Him. My hope is rooted in Him. As I look to the future and wonder – maybe not wonder – as I don't have the capacity quite yet to do that – I know He knows what's best for our family. There's hope, there's peace. Not fear, not anxiety, nor worry. But a knowingness and confidence that He's got this – He's got the best in mind for our family.*

I put my pen to the paper like I have done for many years walking with Him and started to write the words that are more than enough.

"Angela, my beloved daughter, I hold you in the palm of My hands. I am with you and comfort you in your time of loss. My plans for you are good and perfect. My promise is still there. Slow down and give yourself space and grace. Be still and know that I am God. I am for you and your family. Nothing shall come against you. Rest, my child, in My goodness over your life. That is who I am. I am entirely good. If I am for you, who and what can come against you? Rest in My joy, rest in My hope, rest in My peace, Daughter. I give it to you. Walk in it and show and testify of My goodness."

And so with that, I had peace that He knows better than I, so I can trust in His goodness in this difficult situation. I know tears will continue to come in random moments like seeing other pregnant moms, the kids wanting to read a favorite, "God gave us you" book, looking at the drawing Haddie made of our family with the baby that was supposed to be here. I am at peace with the loss as I'm anchored in God's goodness: "Taste and see that the Lord is good; blessed is the one who takes refuge in Him" (Psalms 34:8).

MISCARRIAGE #2: SAMUEL CHENG
JULY 2018

We held onto the promise of having three children and became pregnant two months after our first miscarriage. At that time, we were back in the States for the first time after living in Cambodia for a year and a half. I was two or three months pregnant when it happened again. We had kept this pregnancy quiet and yet were expectant and trusting God. At eight and ten weeks, I went to a clinic to confirm the pregnancy through an ultrasound. The tech saw both times that I was pregnant with an empty sac. She said it could be that or the way the baby was positioned was hard to see. We believed the best and continued on.

I was eleven weeks pregnant and meeting up with a friend at a coffee shop when I started to experience the same symptoms. I drove an hour back to my parents home, singing worship songs to keep my focus. Then there were four hours of cramping, bleeding, sadness and disappointment. This time was quietly shared with our family. I named him Samuel, which in the Bible means "the God who hears." God hears our sadness and disappointment and comforts us in the valley. I made a choice. I will worship Him in the midst of my quiet pain and disappointment and trust in His goodness in this unexpected place again.

MISCARRIAGE #3: ZOE CHENG
MARCH 2019

When I was two months pregnant, I was expectant and believing God that this was the breakthrough of God's promise. We were anticipating what life would look like with a third child, dreamt of going to Thailand to have the baby, and were excited to tell our kids in due time. And then it happened again, I started to bleed off and on for three days. I knew it was the start of another loss. I bled for six hours, visiting the bathroom regularly up and down, while listening to the song *Praise Before My Breakthrough* by Bryan & Katie Towalt. The song and words ministered to me in the midst of living in the tension of not understanding what

I thought was to have been a fulfillment of a promise. I would continue to praise Him in the midst of it because I trusted in God's goodness and faithfulness.

The night of the miscarriage, Thearith and I lit a candle as a symbol of remembrance of the gift I had been carrying. We prayed out our disappointment, celebrated the life I carried for those months, and named the unborn child Zoe. Zoe means *life* in Greek and we named her that because we wanted to honor life. I believe one day in heaven we will meet our children. We prayed, read Scripture together, and ate cake. Cake is part of my grieving process. It's not wine or beer, but there's nothing like a good slice of cake.

That night we read Isaiah 40-41. I found comfort in the question who am I to critique or question God. Isaiah 40:15 states, "The nations are like a drop in the bucket, the coastlands He created like fine dust in His hands, who can compare to Him?" In my wanting to understand why I had experienced another miscarriage, I laid my questions before Him and held on to my Creator, my Sustainer of Life. I held onto a precious verse found in Isaiah 41:10: "For I am your God, I will strength you and help you; I will uphold you with my righteous right hand."

My sister sent me a devotional the night of my miscarriage that I read again and again. It was the story in 2 Kings 6 of how Israel's enemy was trying to kill the prophet Elisha, and his assistant was freaking out about the size of the enemy army that had come against them. Elisha said, "Don't worry. Those who are for us are more than those against us." At first, the assistant didn't see what Elisha was seeing.

How often I have been like that? I don't see how God sees. I see the giant but God sees the stones in David's hands. I see the massive waters and God sees the dry land the Israelites can use to cross over into the land: "Then Elisha prayed, 'O Lord, open his eyes and let him see!' The Lord opened the young man's eyes, and when he looked up, he saw that the hillside around Elisha was filled with horses and chariots of fire" (2 Kings 6:17, NLT).

There was a message in this story for me in this miscarriage. All I was seeing was another loss. Yet I wanted God to show me His perspective of these miscarriages. One afternoon a friend came over with a meal and said she was praying for me at home as she didn't know the words to say to me. She got a sense that there was a "warring'" going on in the heavens about the promise for our family and encouraged me to hold on to hope. It was similar in theme to the 2 Kings Scripture about the Lord's army surrounding them for unseen victory.

She shared with me a couple of songs, one of them *Surrounded* that was inspired from the above portion of Scripture. It is a simple, yet powerful song of when we feel surrounded by negative, we are actually surrounded by Him. She went on to say the exact same words Thearith said to me the night before, "It's not over." God sent her to give me perspective that I was asking for and to renew my heart with hope.

I sometimes wondered what others were thinking as they saw all this. I know I would have thought that we had two wonderful children, so why keep trying? My age, the risk, having had three miscarriages in a year—it seemed foolish to try for more! Then I would remind myself of the Bible stories of prophets doing crazy things out of obedience to God. Things like a teenage gal believing she had conceived Jesus the Son of God by the Holy Spirit; of a battle being won by marching around the walls of Jericho using worship and not swords; of people of God leaving where they were familiar and comfortable to move to foreign, distant lands to share the love of God. All those instances seemed like foolishness in the world's eyes.

God affirmed me in my silence before Him that He saw my beautiful heart believing Him for a word He spoke years ago. In my places of tension, I also thought of Moses who had an intimate friendship with God. He did 'foolish' things out of obedience to God to display that, "Yes, it's for God's glory and has nothing to do with me." Moses saw the Promised Land, but did not get to live in it. So I won't see the fulfillment of some of God's promises this side of life.

With all that in mind, I held onto Him, rather than the gifts or promises He gives or does not give. I praised Him that in my loss, I saw more of Him. I saw His delight in me as His people brought gifts of flowers, meals, and my favorite sweets. All that gave me a deeper knowledge of His character. I would not trade these experiences. They were part of my formation in Him, part of my children's inheritance of deep revelation of who God is so I could tell people later, and give Him glory in the loss.

REFLECTIVE QUESTIONS

1. Grief. Disappointment. Unmet expectations. These are all a part of life. What has helped you cope? How are they similar or different to the ways that I have grieved and processed?

2. What have you learned about God in your grief, disappointment, and unmet expectations? Have you seen His kindness, His comfort? What is holding you back from bringing the hard things to Him?

3. Looking back, describe a time and your perspective about the hard situation you walked through. How did walking through it change you and your perspective of life?

Lord, thank You that You are Lord and can handle the heavy things of life. Thank You that You carry me through when I don't know how to step forward. Thank You for renewing perspective and bringing comfort through Your presence and the love of others. In the spaces and places in my heart that are still heavy and jaded, come and bring healing. I invite You to do so because You are a good, good heavenly Father.

8

THE PROMISE FULFILLED

"For no word from God will ever fail"
(Luke 1:37).

THIRD-BORN:. ZION RASMEY CHENG
JUNE 2020

Zion is my miracle child, my rainbow child, my child promised from God that *causes me to look up and smile towards heaven.* I look at Zion's face and see that the promises of God never fail me. Zion's story actually started for me 13 years earlier when I had an encounter with God during worship, sensing Him speaking to my heart that I would get married and have three children. Being a single missionary in Thailand at that time with no options of potential life partners, this word God spoke to me seemed impossible.

From that time onwards, it was something I believed and trusted that God would do. I wasn't expecting after having Micah that we would walk through the heartache, grief, and loss of three miscarriages. Each of those caused me to question the promise I felt God gave me of having three kids. The miscarriages also took me deeper into the *hope* found in Christ and the *promise* of seeing them and life eternal in God's presence. Physical death, including miscarriages, is not the end but the beginning of something more. It was a difficult but rich time, and I wouldn't trade it for what I received, which was wrestling with those miscarriages and holding on to the promise of seeing our three babies in heaven one day.

God didn't leave me in the dark with my question as to whether we should try again, or if what I heard from God those years ago was true or not. He answered shortly after my third miscarriage. One friend wrote a card stating that she saw me holding a baby, another friend prayed that there was a contending in heaven over the promise.

A couple of months after the third miscarriage, I received some inner healing prayer about the miscarriages while visiting the States. The minister felt God was saying that I was going to receive a 'double portion'; that it wasn't three kids, but rather six! Three were already in heaven and three would be on earth.

A few days later while at a ministry school we were attending, an older lady came up to me and said that she wanted to pray for me. She had this impression of labor pains and also had the impression of the number "three" and asked if I had two kids already and wanted another. I said yes and then she prayed over me to get pregnant. Only God can be so specific. He is such a personal, relational God. After those encounters, along with God speaking to my heart that the promise is still valid, I had courage for us to keep trying for number three on earth.

Let's fast forward a couple of months when we were back in Cambodia and I found out I had skin cancer. I needed to take a week-long trip solo to Bangkok to have skin surgery on my face while Thearith and the two kids stayed behind. With all the arrangements of that and starting homeschooling for the kids, we weren't thinking about getting pregnant. But what a surprising gift it was when I was in Bangkok for surgery prep and found out I was pregnant.

My pregnancy with Zion seemed to fly by as I spent my days chasing after the kids. I had more energy than the other two pregnancies. I attributed that to the significant lifestyle change I made to plant-based eating and juicing to help bring healing to my body with the skin cancer.

Another unexpected surprise came with Zion. We were planning on having Zion delivered in Bangkok, due to limited medical resources in Cambodia for a high-risk pregnancy like mine. Our plans changed in mid-March 2020 when we decided to come to the States. The global pandemic was causing border closings and limiting international travel. We decided over a two-day period to buy tickets, pack up the house, and go to Wisconsin to have the baby.

With that decision came many unknowns of how long we would be here, how health insurance would work, and where would provision for our various needs come from. It caused us to trust in God's faithfulness, combating worry and anxiety by thanking God daily for the things we often took for granted. Staying at my parents on their farm gave us the quiet, space, nature, and family connection during the months of waiting and social distancing.

The week of my due date, I started having constant contractions. At the same time, the dermatologist called regarding a biopsy from a suspicious black mole on my leg. He said it was melanoma stage zero and he wanted to take it out within two weeks. So the day before my due date, I had skin surgery, requiring a six-centimeter incision on my upper leg to remove melanoma. I began to pray that I would have a few days to heal before birthing Zion because I preferred to sway, stand, and walk through contractions. The timing was perfect as Zion came five days after my due date.

With Micah, I was close to giving birth in the car or parking lot, so this time I wanted to get to the hospital earlier! We went in shortly after I started having consistent contractions. I ended up laboring two hours at the hospital. I cried tears of joy when I saw Zion, a long-awaited gift. His full name is Zion Rasmey Cheng. Zion is a common word used in the Bible that refers to the heavenly city.

We believe that Zion will be a man who will cause people to look at things above and not things of this earth. There is so much more to come than what we see in the natural. The best is yet to come—eternity with Christ: "Think about the things of heaven, not the things of earth" (Colossians 3:2). Rasmey *(pronounce RA-smay)* is a Cambodian name that means light and sunshine. We believe Zion will bring God's light into the darkness. He will be sunshine after times of mourning and loss.

What a journey it was seeing this promise of God come to pass in my life. It reminds me of the Israelites who were promised a land filled with milk and honey. They walked through the desert for years, questioned the Lord, and fought many battles during the journey to the promise. It was far from easy. The Lord was with them the entire time shaping and guiding them into the promise.

I love how in this verse the hard things of life happen, yet I can walk through them because He walks with me through them: "When you're in over your head, I'll be there with you. When you're in rough waters, you will not go down. When you're between a rock and a hard place, it won't be a dead end—because I am God, your personal God, the Holy One of Israel, your Savior" (Isaiah 43:2-3, MSG).

REFLECTIVE QUESTIONS

1. Reflect on a time when you were believing for a promise from God that involved waiting, momentary suffering, and/or contending in faith. What lessons did you learn?

2. What is something that you are waiting for God to fulfill?

Lord, to wait on You is to have confident expectation in Your love and goodness. Your plans, ways, timing and thoughts are better than my best. Your word says that "I don't think the way you think. The way you work isn't the way I work. God's decrees. For as the sky soars high above the earth, so the way I work surpasses the way you work, and the way I think is beyond the way you think" (Isaiah 55:8-9, MSG). In my waiting, I trust in Your word, promises, and goodness.

9

SEPARATED AT A CAMBODIAN AIRPORT

"He knows us far better than we know
ourselves. That's why we can be so sure
that every detail in our lives of love for
God is worked into something good"
(Romans 8:27-28, MSG).

My baby and I were in our emptied apartment in Cambodia, another unexpected place where we experienced God's goodness. I was questioning, *When will we be reunited with the rest of my family? Do I have enough clothes, diapers, and essentials in the random totes I grabbed in the frantic time at the airport before my hubby took the rest of our fifteen bags?* Hours earlier we were told our baby couldn't board the plane. Legs shaking, shocked like a deer in headlights, we made fast decisions and were separated. Baby Zion and I would stay in Cambodia and the rest of the family would fly to the U.S.

Let me backtrack a bit. Three months after Zion was born in America, we went through the stressful process of global travel with three little ones. We wanted to return back to our home in Cambodia. Traveling is tiring. Traveling with littles is a test of patience on a 30-hour door-to-door trip with heaps of suitcases needed for our next term overseas in a developing country. Add on top of that COVID travel with constantly changing airline protocols including COVID testing requirements from country to country.

However, we were willing to do what it took since we wanted to get back to our home and our apartment, to the space in Asia that my kids called home. The capital city of Phnom Penh had been our home for four years. We thought we were going to be there for a year and half before we would move back to U.S. for good. However, that timeline wasn't God's timeline, because our leave date got pushed up.

Since arriving back to Cambodia, COVID restrictions continued to get tighter. As the capital navigated COVID, the city became zoned into areas not allowing you to cross into other parts. There was a nightly curfew for months, and if you got COVID, you would be escorted away to a government facility. We were stuck in our high-rise apartments for months, making the best of it. We prayed and fasted and felt that we should bump up our timeline of when we would move back to the States. Packing, donating, and selling within a three-week window before we left were not easy to do.

Within a week, I sold 300 items on Facebook Marketplace using scooter taxis to deliver as travel was prohibited between zones. We booked tickets back to the U.S. through an agent in case we would have trouble, but we along with our agent overlooked something.

U.S. customs said babies two and under didn't need a COVID test upon arrival to the States but we had a connecting flight in Taiwan. Taiwan had changed their rule, saying all transit passengers needed a test. I stood in shock at the check-in counter with our three littles and our huge mess of bags, stroller, car seats, and travel pack 'n play. What would we do? Thearith made the wise decision with which I agreed for he and the two older kids to board and I stayed back with the baby. We neither wanted to drag all our stuff back to an empty apartment, nor go through the expense and stress of rebooking tickets and COVID tests.

We are never alone. God always has our back. I experienced that time and time again as I've traveled on mission to remote areas, hard places, and foreign lands. I called our apartment landlord and they graciously said I could come back and stay in our empty apartment as long as I needed for free. Neighbors, church family, and our pastor were there to give me hugs, buy food, and lend me essentials when arriving back to the empty apartment!

It ended up that extra week in Cambodia turned out to be a gift to me. From the moment we decided we were leaving, it was all-consuming. I was on overdrive, functioning on adrenaline, stressed, and sleep deprived. I was so absorbed in the details, including my kids bucket list of who they wanted to see before we left, that I hadn't even thought of my bucket list or of emotionally saying goodbye to people and places.

That week was for me. I had morning walks in our neighborhood to say goodbye, saw friends who prayed with me, and had sweet times of fellowship with the Lord. One morning, God told me to get a cake from my favorite Japanese bakery. That night after I put my baby to sleep, I ate my cake and felt the Lord ask me if would I give Southeast Asia back to Him. I cried and cried because Southeast Asia had been a part of my heart and identity for 20 years. As I did, He gave me promises for the new seasons ahead. What a gift!

I'm so glad the Father had us bump up our timelines since the year ahead of us would see both my husband and I on the brink of death. We wouldn't have had the medical resources needed to see us through the unexpected storms. The Father sees our future as well as our present. His ways and thoughts are higher and far better than ours.

REFLECTIVE QUESTIONS

1. Think back on a time in your life when God turned a bad situation into something good. Give Him thanks that He works all things for the good of those who love Him.

2. What are the gifts, as I call them, that you have received when things didn't turn out the way you envisioned them to go? Thank the Lord for His kindness and presence.

Lord, You have seen me through thick and thin. How grateful I am that there is no place that You are not with me. Thank You that nothing, absolutely nothing, can separate me from Your love. Whenever I call upon Your name, You show up. Your peace and presence stabilize me like a boat that is anchored within deep, deep waters.

10

A HOME IN THE U.S.

"And my God will meet all your needs
according to the riches of his glory in
Christ Jesus" (Philippians 4:19).

Never did I think we would own a home in America. Living in America had never been my desire. I had seen our lives being lived out in the nations, in the majority world. During the pandemic, I felt a nudge inside of me that we should root our family in the States in years to come and buy a home. What Lord? Buy a home? Where would we get that kind of money to do that as volunteer missionaries?

In the months of waiting to go back to Cambodia after Zion was born, together we started praying and discerning God's will about this. That lead to our family taking a scouting trip before we went back to Cambodia. We were looking for a YWAM ministry in the States that worked with Asian refugees and served low-income areas reaching out to children and families. We found all that in YWAM-Pittsburgh. Their leadership team and we both sensed that our family joining their team was the next move for us.

The Bible has become my daily bread for

the last twenty years. A lot of times the Lord will lead me and confirm things to me when I open up His Word. While nursing a newborn, I wasn't in the Word and had asked God to confirm to me in some random way that Pittsburgh was for us. It was a big move for our family from Southeast Asia to Pittsburgh. It was also a city where we didn't have family and didn't know anyone.

The very next day after that scouting trip, I was sitting on my parent's rocker to nurse Zion. I put on *Sesame Street* for the kids to watch when my daughter said, "Look, Mom, this is where we just visited." Big Bird had gone on a field trip to Pittsburgh and was visiting Pittsburgh landmarks. God will speak to us through dreams, through His Word, through other believers, and through Big Bird on Sesame Street. We then knew Pittsburgh was on the horizon. I started dreaming with God about all it would entail—asking God for His heart and vision for us, dreaming about what I wanted in a home, and praying for all the logistics and fundraising needed for this global move.

My family and I have seen how the Lord provides time and time again for the little and big needs both for us and those we serve. Our biggest stretch of faith thus far was this one. We needed cars, insurance, winter clothes, $1,000 more in monthly support to live in America, a large sum of money for a down payment, and all that one needs to put in a home. And God did it all through our global church family.

As we prayed, as we connected with our donors and family of believers, the Lord provided more than $65,000 in 60 days, along with a minivan for *free* from one of our donors. We were able to buy a home for less than the asking price during a booming housing market. The owner even included a lawn mower, bedroom furniture, and snow blower when he heard we were missionaries and needed to fill an empty home.

After many years of sleeping under mosquito net coverings in various nations, on church pews or villages, and going back and forth between countries, I was ready to have a place to call home. It is still surreal and brings tears to my eyes, praising God for those who gave to see this lofty dream happen. Only the Lord could do that. Neither T nor I are eloquent, and we are not high pressure or inspirational in what we say to see the provision come in through our asking. We asked a church family to continue to partner with us in the ministry we felt the Lord was leading us to in Pittsburgh. It's a humbling experience to ask to have your needs met. Let me tell you more about that.

I grew up in with the family value where we worked hard to provide for our family, only spend what we had. When I said yes to missions, it also meant saying yes to trusting the Lord for my salary, later my family's salary, and for the ministry expenses of those we served. That was a huge step of faith as well as a humbling one. Within our mission organization, every YWAM volunteer, including the founder, Loren Cunningham, raises funds to meet their own financial needs. For most people, these funds come from friends, family, and churches.

YWAM has intentionally chosen to emphasize personal support raising as the primary means of funding for their staff. Although we recognize that there are many other valid ways of financing ministry, we believe the way we have chosen is based on biblical principles. Just as the staff of a church or a community service organization relies on donations to pay their salary, YWAM staff also rely on financial partners to meet their personal and ministry needs. Some biblical examples of living by faith are as follows:

- Levites (Numbers 18:24): The Levites received a promise of the tithe instead of land. They were born into this calling and didn't have a tribal inheritance. When God selected the Levites for special service, He already had the tithe in mind as the means through which they would be supported.
- Jesus (Matthew 10:9-10; Luke 8:2-3): Jesus was supported by personal gifts from others. He wasn't underwritten by a religious body and didn't work an outside job. He and His team were supported by the gifts of a group of followers.

Living out dreams from God involves others. It also requires looking up and believing God, while looking around us and inviting others to be involved. I do my part by taking the steps forward in faith, trusting the Lord in the process. I have seen that to be true in fifteen years of living by faith as a missionary and in the unexpected dream of owning a home.

REFLECTIVE QUESTIONS

1. When's the last time you asked, of God or others, for help, for prayer, for support to do something you could not do yourself? How does it feel to ask compared to being the one who is helping someone else who asked? Step out and ask to have a need met because it brings joy to others who help you. We were meant to receive as well as give.

2. What is a dream you have that seems impossible? Don't give up; we have a God who does abundantly more than what we can dream or imagine.

3. All Christ's followers are called to be a part of missions. What do you sense your role is? To give, to go, and/or to pray for those who go?

Lord, thank You for always providing everything I need: clean water, shelter, food, family, education, the ability to read and write. My list could go on for pages of Your goodness. Lord, I know and have seen that these gifts are not a reality for many around the world. Thank You for the privilege it has been to give and be a part of meeting others' needs. Thank You for all the times I have asked and others have given to my needs. Every good and perfect gift comes from You. Remind me to be grateful for the simple, the small, and the big gifts in my daily life. I commit to give to those in need so that basic needs can be met. Don't allow me to ever take for granted that You are the source of meeting all my needs. Help me to not be stingy or apathetic. I know I can never out-give You.

11

INSIDE THE INTENSIVE CARE UNIT

"For we live by faith, not by sight"
(2 Corinthians 5:7).

Having put on the protective COVID hospital gown, face shield, and plastic gloves, I entered the room where my husband lay connected to high flow oxygen. I put socks on my husband feet since he couldn't move or stand. An old Jewish ICU doctor came in to have a talk with me. He wanted to ask if I would consent to allow my husband to be on a ventilator if need be. I looked in his tired eyes as he said it had been a long night in the unit. I could sense someone had passed away the night before in the COVID ICU unit.

Before we went on talking, I asked if I could lay my hand on his shoulder to pray for him. My heart began to fill with compassion for all those working tirelessly through the pandemic. There I was in the presence of hospital workers that I had seen on the news for months. Compassion has a face. Being there in the trenches, surrounded by the intensity of it with my beloved husband not in a good state, motivated me to look only to God to pull us through this storm of COVID. I had never been in an ICU room nor did I expect I would be there in my first weeks in Pittsburgh. I guess none of us expect the worst, right?

A week after moving to a new city in our home, both my husband and I contracted COVID. We weren't even unpacked fully. I didn't have many symptoms, other than fatigue and brain fog. Over the days, however, my husband got progressively worse. Six days into worsening symptoms, I hauled him with my three littles to the ER. I couldn't go in and dropped him off even though he wasn't fully coherent, not knowing what was going to happen. That was difficult.

A few hours later he called to say he was discharged so I packed up the kids and went back to pick him up that night. I didn't sleep at all since I was filled with anxiety and fear as I listened to him breathe. The next morning when I checked his oximeter levels and they were once again low, I loaded up the kids again and went to a different ER, one that our team leaders said would allow the children and I to be in there. It was rough seeing him connected to machines while waiting in the ER to see how things were going to proceed.

In our waiting room sat next to me an anxious woman who I learned was about to have heart surgery. She was alone, so I asked if I could pray for her. In our weakest human moments, what gifts presence and care are to receive and give. As I said earlier, perhaps the most powerful ministry I have given and received is that ministry of presence—of being with someone in their weak moments.

Thearith was admitted and that night was moved to ICU. Overnight, his condition worsened and he was put on high flow oxygen. I could have lost him at home if we had not gone into the hospital. Those were scary days. However, our families were amazing. His sister flew in from Los Angeles the day he was admitted. I had been solo parenting for a week and a half trying to hold it together, living on adrenaline and no sleep. Her presence and help were God sent.

My family brought up the idea of them helping with the kids. It was a hard decision to have my family split up again, but I knew I needed to do it so I could focus solely on advocating and being fully present with Thearith. My parents came to pick up Haddie and Micah while my one-year-old stayed with me since I was still nursing him.

During this time, I was constantly dialoging with the Lord. I started posting daily updates and prayer requests on social media to rally God's people to contend in prayer to see healing so I could bring Thearith home. The Lord put on my heart to connect with four specific friends who are medically informed that I could message to get input on medical decisions I needed to make. I had learned while in Asia that we need to be our own advocate and be involved in the process. No one cares more about your loved one or your health than you do.

I cried out to the Lord while blaring my worship music on the way to the hospital every morning. I felt the intensity of the atmosphere that first day in ICU. Instead of the presence of fear and death there, I wanted to carry in God's peace, love, hope, and faith. I would pray in the Spirit, visually putting on the armor of God, having focused my attention on God through worship before I entered. Thearith said I was like the preacher who came in every morning. I had a worship song ready for us, or I should say for me to sing followed by reading the Word of God over him.

Worship and the Word shift atmospheres. That is what I wanted to do during the allotted visitors' hour (that I constantly tried extending). After every visit, I waited outside to talk to his nurses, I asked to see his standard of care papers daily, and said yes and no to drugs they wanted to give. Though my husband lay before me connected to many wires and loud machines, all I knew to do was hold onto God's Word. The Word of God is our medicine, so to speak. By God's Word, He created all that we see so when we profess His Word, He acts.

> Then you called out to GOD in your desperate condition; He got you out in the nick of time. He spoke the Word that healed you, that pulled you back from the brink of death. So thank God for His marvelous love, for his miracle mercy to the children He loves; Offer thanksgiving sacrifices, tell the world what He's done—sing it out! (Psalm 107:19-21, MSG).

One particular morning, Thearith was struggling quite a bit and called me to come in earlier. The Lord gave me the idea to bring in our wedding and kids albums to look through the pictures with him. Thearith is a picture man. He loves taking photos to capture life's moments. He says looking through them that morning motivated him to persevere. He said that when death was right before him, life became real simple. Flashing before him was his life of work, the ministry, the trips, the stuff—all of that didn't matter. He learned all that mattered was living for the Lord, our families, and our kids.

After visiting him one afternoon, I went out to buy a dinner table. Yep, a dinner table that by faith I was going to see my family reunited and sit together for years to come celebrating the Lord's goodness. Having just moved, we didn't have a dinner table, nor at that present moment did I have my family to put around it.

Speaking of goodness, can I boast for a moment about the goodness of the local church? We hadn't even been to a church in our new city and yet during this crisis, we had meals being dropped off, people who came to mow my lawn, unpack, and assemble house appliances I had in the garage. And Christians around the world were praying for complete healing.

Eventually, we saw the major breakthrough we had been believing God for and one day with his need for oxygen dropped significantly, followed by the next day when he was out of ICU. He spent 11 days in the hospital followed by a couple weeks at home with an oxygen tank just in case I saw his oxygen drop. Our kids came back the week after and we were all united sitting around the dinner table I had bought, feasting on the Lord's goodness.

REFLECTIVE QUESTIONS

1. The ministry of presence was a huge help in crisis to lighten the load. When have you given or received the ministry of presence— someone being there for you or you being there for someone in one of life's darkest hours?

2. "Taste and see that the Lord is good, blessed is the one who takes refuge in Him" (Psalm 34:8). When was a time you took refuge in the Lord and found His goodness?

Praise You Lord that You are a living God. You are the same yesterday, today, and forever. I call upon Your name and You answer me. You are my deliverer and healer. You give me wisdom when I ask, You guide me in the chaos, and You send help when the load is too big. You alone are worthy to be praised!

12

WALKING THROUGH CANCER

"Beloved daughter, your faith in me
released your healing. You may go with
my peace" (Luke 8:48).

The month after Thearith got out of ICU, my own personal bomb exploded. I found out I had aggressive melanoma cancer in my lymph system. My first Thanksgiving back in the States, I found myself having neck surgery to remove the lymph nodes where I had found a lump, followed by a couple more surgeries. The cancer diagnosis started a great pause for us that led us to make radical changes in our life to aid in healing and recovering from the shellshock of cancer, transition, trauma, and grief.

Our family had just driven to Colorado for a family missionary debriefing week to help us work through grief, loss, and unpack our overseas stories. It was really a sweet time when we built in a week for visiting friends and taking in the beauty of Colorado. During the debriefing, we drew a picture of where we currently were at emotionally. I drew a bomb ready to burst.

I had been holding it all together for my family during so many unexpected events the past years. Being displaced out of our Cambodian home and life rhythm during COVID; lacking community and the loss that it had caused; years of lack of sleep from nursing babies; the miscarriages; packing our lives and home in three weeks during the pandemic lockdown in Cambodia; the stress of fundraising for living in America; the trauma of losing control of our car on our way to house hunt in Pittsburgh; and most recently the trauma of Thearith being near death, all created intense pressure that made me feel like a bomb ready to explode. And guess what? It did!

Before I continue, I must say we all have sayings we utter when we don't know what else to say. One of those sayings is, "God won't give more than you can handle or bear." Well, I learned that's bogus! I was definitely at a place where I couldn't take any more unexpected curve balls and then I got another—the cancer diagnosis. What I can testify to is that the saying should be more like, "God will carry us through when we are in over our heads with more than we can handle and bear."

As we started our 21-hour road trip back to Pittsburgh after our debriefing, I felt and saw a visible lump on my neck when I went in to use the gas station bathroom. Could it be a swollen lymph node from all the stress I had been under? Could it be something more? My mind was all over the place and sitting in a car for hours on end didn't help. On the drive, I called an ENT doctor, pushed a bit about the urgency, and got an appointment for the next day when I had a needle biopsy. A couple days later, I got the doctor's call saying it was melanoma. He was ordering MRI and PET scans to see if and to where it had spread.

I was filled with fear and anxiety, along with waves of God's peace. I woke up in fear almost every night for a month. I took the time to research my options conventionally and alternatively, connected with other melanoma survivors in the States, got second and third opinions from different doctors, and cried out for God's help. One day, I was going to a clinic in Mexico for treatment; the next day I was doing surgery. I was like a deer in headlights—shocked and indecisive.

Looking back, the Lord carried me through and put the right decisions and counsel around me. Thearith was *amazing*. He was anchor for our kids and me while I was in my shocked stage. The day after diagnosis, I put pen to the paper like I've done for years to hear what my heavenly Father wanted to say. How assuring to hear the voice of our Lord. He wants to comfort us and speak to us in the storms. He will be with us to get us through them. Here is what I heard:

> *Angela, my beloved, chosen and accepted daughter of the King. This didn't catch me by surprise. I AM—with you! Your healer, your counselor, your great advocate. This is for you—your healing and recovery. Rest in My presence. I AM Creator. I AM your Source. I AM your Deliverer. Can I lead you, Daughter, in this unexpected dance? Do not fear. I AM with you. I will uphold you with My righteous right hand.*

I replied, "Lord, lead me to the right resources, lead me to the right people. I trust you.

You have always been faithful. You are my source."

Two days after my diagnosis, Thearith and I went into the prayer room at the church we had just started attending. I sobbed like a baby in the arms of the pastor, asking him to call the elders together to pray for me. They did and one of them shared the story of Jesus' healing a woman found in Luke 8:43-48. She had been subject to bleeding for twelve years and nothing could heal her. With noise, chaos, and crowds around her, she thought to herself, *If only I will touch the cloak of Jesus, I would be healed.* That is just what she did. She reached out to touch the cloak of Jesus and was completely healed. She believed in her mind before she saw with her eyes that a touch from Jesus would bring her healing. Luke 8:48 became my anchor through the storm of cancer.

I sought the Lord and He answered me, giving me promises to claim. "Beloved Daughter, your faith in Me released your healing. Now go in peace." I believed from the get go that my body was in the hands of the Lord as my Master Physician and Healer, who has the amazing ability to heal not only physically, but also emotionally and spiritually. He was able to heal my whole person.

The Word of God has the power to heal and His Word became my anchor like never before. I've seen Him heal and had experienced it before, so my words were going to anchored in His Word. I also decided I was going to choose to be grateful and joyful. I decided that whatever new healing-at-home rhythms were required, I was going to accept them with joy, and in the days ahead, we made radical changes to reduce my stress load.

Some of those radical changes were deciding to put our kids right away in a private Christian school. I had been homeschooling them and knew that with my new healing regimen, we needed to take that off my plate. Anything that was causing me stress had to go. Watching the news and social media were eliminated. I knew I needed grief and trauma counseling and started to pray and look for emotional healing counseling. I needed to start to slow down my body from fight-or-flight mode so I could enter rest-and-recovery mode.

Each morning upon waking, I took my daily medicine: spending time in the Word of God. I journaled at least three things I was thankful for to start my day. Thearith started to do the nighttime wake-ups for our one year old and mornings with the kids so I could focus on getting better sleep and healing. He bought me a second-hand fridge to store all the organic produce I was going to be eating and juicing. Overnight, I radically changed what I ate.

The Lord placed a beacon of hope in my life in the person of a cancer coach who had been healed from melanoma cancer. She was a source of counsel in deciding on what treatment plan I was going to deploy. My mom-in-law came and stayed with us for four months. What a *huge* gift of support for our family while I had three surgeries and introduced all the new healing rhythms in our home.

With healing from cancer, I am reminded that every baby step forward, every detox I do, every living, nutritious food I choose to eat, every walk in nature, every counseling session is one small step to recovering my life. The Lord holds the number of days in His hand. I am going to do all that I can to feed my mind, body, and spirit with good and the truth that leads to abundant life. I shall not look too far off in the distance to wonder how long that will be. Instead, I joyfully take the baby steps forward that bring me health and healing. I choose to live in gratitude with eyes and heart focused on eternity.

REFLECTIVE QUESTIONS

1. Storms and unexpected events come in our lives. What are the anchors that can see you through the unexpected storms? Have there been specific Bible verses you cling to, wise counselors around you, and/or the sweet presence of God?

2. James 4:8 says draw near to God and He will draw near to you. The invitation is always there to talk to Him. Ask your heavenly Father for what you need. Ask for help. He promises to draw near and carry us through the fires of life.

*Lord, I mediate on the truth of
Psalms 121:1-8:*

*I lift my eyes to the mountains—where
does my help come from?
My help comes from the Lord, the
Maker of heaven and earth.
He will not let your foot slip—he who
watches over you will not slumber;
Indeed, he who watches over Israel will
never slumber or sleep.'
The Lord watches over you- the Lord is
your shade at your right hand;
the sun will not harm you by day, nor
the moon by night.
The Lord will keep you from all harm—
He will watch over your life;
the Lord will watch over your coming
and going both now and forevermore.*

13

HOME

"Don't let your heart be troubled. You
believe in God; believe also in me. My
Father's house has many rooms; if that
were not so, would I have told you that
I am going there to prepare a place for
you? And if I go and prepare a place for
you, I will come back and take you to be
with me that you also may be where I
am. You know the way to the place where
I am going" (John 14:1-4).

"I am the way, the truth, and the Life.
No one comes to the Father except
through me" (John 14:6).

My perspective of home has shifted with
all the unexpected places where I've lived. My
childhood home in farmland Wisconsin is home
to me; Thailand and Cambodia are home to me;
and now Pittsburgh is home to me. These places
have people who are near and dear to my heart.
These homes have shaped and changed me.
I love to describe *home* as a place people are
waiting for you. In those places there are people
and memories of endearment.

Of all the places I've called home, there's
only one place I've not yet been to: my eternal

home in heaven. The Creator of heaven and earth, the Lover of my soul, God the Father, Son, and Holy Spirit is waiting for me and preparing my place. He has changed me and my identity in so many ways over the years. I've set my gaze on eternity. I look white on the outside, but I am Wisconsin, Asian, and eternity-focused on the inside.

Jesus promises that He is preparing a room for me. I imagine that my banqueting table will have the best Thai papaya salad and sticky rice, some more sticky rice and mango, and a fine piece of vegan cheesecake for dessert. My room will be like a garden with the most beautiful smells and colors, filled with an array of exotic flowers and greens. It will be the most glorious and peaceful home.

And there I will behold Him: the Creator of heaven and earth. I cannot even start to imagine what that will be like. To see loved ones who have gone before me, as well as the heroes of the faith in the Bible. Will I talk with Queen Esther, David, and Father Abraham? The Lord or His angels will come back to take my spirit to glory when it's my time. He is the Way, the Truth and the *Life*, and those that believe in Him will have eternal life.

> "Look God has moved into the neighborhood, making his home with men and women! They're His people, He's their God. He will wipe every tear of their eyes. Death is gone for good—tears are gone, crying gone, pain gone" (Revelation 21:3-4, MSG).

Often I've thought of being at home with Christ. What I mean by that is my heart is at rest with the inner peace of knowing the presence of God through the Holy Spirit who is living in me. I've felt His peace through the valleys and the mountaintop experiences. His presence has given me the courage to take Him at His Word and go to the places and people He's led me to. His peace and presence sustain me. There's no place I have been where He has not been there with me.

How about you? Have you made room in your heart to allow the Prince of Peace in? Our days on earth are numbered. Our sin prevents us from experiencing this peace and presence of God. But what joy it is that the gift of God is eternal life. Jesus made the way by His sacrifice and victorious resurrection on the cross. He thought of you before the foundations of the earth with the plan of sending Himself to earth because He couldn't bear being eternally separated from you.

What is your best example of love? Has anyone ever loved you so much that they would die in your place when you didn't even have any kind of connection with them? There's no greater love than that, right? There is no better example of what love is and what it looks like than Christ's love for you. He loves you like no other human.

> "So this is my command: Love each other deeply, as much as I have loved you. For the greatest love of all is a love that sacrifices all. And this great love is demonstrated when a person sacrifices his life for his friends" (John 15:12-13, TPT).

God is love, a perfect love with no strings attached. He gives and gives and gives some more. The biggest decision you'll ever make that carries the weight of where your home for eternity is rests on if you choose to receive His Love shown through Jesus. If you do, you are adopted as an heir, a son or daughter of the King, and you receive the gift of the Holy Spirit that abides in those who receive the gift of salvation. You become royalty because the King of kings and Lord of lords is your heavenly Father.

- "Teach us to number our days, that we may gain a heart of wisdom" (Psalm 90:12).

- "For all have sinned and fall short of the glory of God" (Romans 3:23).

- "For the wages of sin is death, but the gift of God is eternal life in Christ our Lord" (Romans 6:23).

- "For if you declare with your mouth that Jesus is Lord and believe in your heart that God raised him from the dead, you will experience salvation. The heart that believes in him receives the gift of righteousness of God—and then the mouth confesses, resulting in salvation. For the Scriptures encourages us with these words: 'everyone who believes in Him will never be disappointed'" (Romans 10:9-11).

It's easy, my friend, to receive the gift. All you need to do is open your hands and heart to receive it. All you need to do is say, *God, I don't understand it all but today I want to receive Your perfect love. I want my home to be secure in heaven. Thank You, Jesus, for standing in my place of sin and death. Lead my life. Come make Your home in me.* If you said that for the first time, tell someone you know who is a Christian you did, or reach out to connect with me and start connecting and growing in your understanding of who God is.

If you made it this far, thank you for sacrificing your time and reading God's story that has played out in my life. My aim is to testify of the Lord's goodness in my journey and to perhaps cause you to see and dream of the Lord's goodness operating in yours.

This is us.

If you want to stay connected to my family ministry and me, or wish to contribute to our ministry, please email me at

happybcuz@yahoo.com

Made in the USA
Monee, IL
20 October 2023